Grayslake Area Public Library District
Grayslake, Illinois

WEEKLY **WR** READER®
EARLY LEARNING LIBRARY

+ SAFETY / LA SEGURIDAD
FIRST / ES LO PRIMERO

Staying Safe / La seguridad
At School / en la escuela

by/por Joanne Mattern

Reading consultant/Consultora de lectura: Susan Nations, M.Ed.,
author, literacy coach, consultant in literacy development/
autora, tutora de alfabetización, consultora de desarrollo de la lectura

Please visit our web site at: www.garethstevens.com
For a free color catalog describing Weekly Reader® Early Learning Library's list
of high-quality books, call 1-877-445-5824 (USA) or 1-800-387-3178 (Canada).
Weekly Reader® Early Learning Library's fax: (414) 336-0164.

Library of Congress Cataloging-in-Publication Data available upon request from publisher.
Fax (414) 336-0157 for the attention of the Publishing Records Department.

ISBN-13: 978-0-8368-8057-1 (lib. bdg.)
ISBN-13: 978-0-8368-8064-9 (softcover)

This edition first published in 2007 by
Weekly Reader® Early Learning Library
A Member of the WRC Media Family of Companies
330 West Olive Street, Suite 100
Milwaukee, WI 53212 USA

Managing editor: Valerie J. Weber
Editor: Barbara Kiely Miller
Art direction: Tammy West
Cover design and page layout: Charlie Dahl
Picture research: Diane Laska-Swanke
Photographer: Jack Long
Spanish translation: Tatiana Acosta and Guillermo Gutiérrez

Printed in the United States of America

1 2 3 4 5 6 7 8 9 10 10 09 08 07 06

Note to Educators and Parents

Reading is such an exciting adventure for young children! They are beginning to integrate their oral language skills with written language. To encourage children along the path to early literacy, books must be colorful, engaging, and interesting; they should invite the young reader to explore both the print and the pictures.

The *Safety First* series is designed to help young readers review basic safety rules, learn new vocabulary, and strengthen their reading comprehension. In simple, easy-to-read language, each book teaches children to stay safe in an everyday situation such as at home, school, or in the outside world.

Each book is specially designed to support the young reader in the reading process. The familiar topics are appealing to young children and invite them to read — and reread — again and again. The full-color photographs and enhanced text further support the student during the reading process.

In addition to serving as wonderful picture books in schools, libraries, homes, and other places where children learn to love reading, these books are specifically intended to be read within an instructional guided reading group. This small group setting allows beginning readers to work with a fluent adult model as they make meaning from the text. After children develop fluency with the text and content, the book can be read independently. Children and adults alike will find these books supportive, engaging, and fun!

— Susan Nations, M.Ed., author/literacy coach/
and consultant in literacy development

Nota para los maestros y los padres

¡Leer es una aventura tan emocionante para los niños pequeños! A esta edad están comenzando a integrar su manejo del lenguaje oral con el lenguaje escrito. Para animar a los niños en el camino de la lectura incipiente, los libros deben ser coloridos, estimulantes e interesantes; deben invitar a los jóvenes lectores a explorar la letra impresa y las ilustraciones.

La seguridad es lo primero es una nueva colección diseñada para ayudar a los jóvenes lectores a repasar normas de seguridad básicas, aprender vocabulario nuevo y reforzar su comprensión de la lectura. Con un lenguaje sencillo y fácil de leer, cada libro enseña a los niños cómo estar seguros en situaciones de la vida diaria en casa, la escuela o cuando salen de paseo.

Cada libro está especialmente diseñado para ayudar a los jóvenes lectores en el proceso de lectura. Los temas familiares llaman la atención de los niños y los invitan a leer una y otra vez. Las fotografías a todo color y el tamaño de la letra ayudan aún más al estudiante en el proceso de lectura.

Además de servir como maravillosos libros ilustrados en escuelas, bibliotecas, hogares y otros lugares donde los niños aprenden a amar la lectura, estos libros han sido especialmente concebidos para ser leídos en un grupo de lectura guiada. Este contexto permite que los lectores incipientes trabajen con un adulto que domina la lectura mientras van determinando el significado del texto. Una vez que los niños dominan el texto y el contenido, el libro puede ser leído de manera independiente. ¡Estos libros les resultarán útiles, estimulantes y divertidos a niños y a adultos por igual!

— Susan Nations, M.Ed., autora/tutora de
alfabetización/consultora de desarrollo de la lectura

Do you know how to stay safe at school?

¿Sabes cómo mantener la seguridad en la escuela?

Do not run in the halls. Stay
in line and do not push.

— — — — — — — — — — — — — —

No corras en los pasillos.
Avanza en fila y sin empujar.

Be careful when you carry things. Carry scissors with the sharp end pointing down.

- - - - - - - - - - - - - -

Presta atención cuando lleves cosas. Lleva las tijeras con la punta afilada apuntando hacia el suelo.

9

A **fire drill** lets you **practice** how to get out of school safely if there is a fire. Listen for the **alarm**.

Un **simulacro de incendio** te permite **practicar** cómo salir de la escuela con seguridad si hay un fuego. Escucha la **alarma**.

During a fire drill, you must leave the school. Do not run or talk.

- - - - - - - - - - - - - - -

Durante un simulacro de incendio, debes salir de la escuela. No te pongas a correr ni a hablar.

Follow the rules at **recess**.
Wait for your turn. Watch
out for other children playing.

— — — — — — — — — — — —

En el **recreo**, respeta las reglas.
Espera a que sea tu turno. Ten
cuidado con los demás niños que
están jugando.

Tell a teacher if someone gets hurt. The school nurse will help.

- - - - - - - - - - - -

Avisa a una maestra si alguien se hace daño. La enfermera de la escuela está allí para ayudar.

Some children might try to hurt others. These children are called **bullies**. Tell a teacher if someone is acting like a bully.

— — — — — — — — — — — — —

Algunos niños podrían tratar de hacer daño a los demás. Estos son **niños abusivos**. Avisa a una maestra si algún niño está siendo abusivo.

Everyone at school works together to make school a safe place!

- - - - - - - - - - - - - -

¡Todos colaboran para que la escuela sea un lugar seguro!

125B
PRINCIPAL

Glossary

alarm — a sound, light, or other signal that warns people about danger

bullies — people who are mean to other people or who try to hurt them

fire drill — the practice of the right way to get out of a building in case of a fire

practice — to repeat something many times so you can get better at it

recess — a short time to rest or play during the day

Glosario

alarma — sonido, luz u otra señal que advierte a las personas del peligro

niños abusivos — niños que se comportan mal con los demás o que tratan de hacerles daño

practicar — hacer algo varias veces para mejorar

recreo — periodo corto del día para descansar o jugar

simulacro de incendio — práctica de la manera correcta de salir de un edificio en caso de incendio

For More Information/Más información

Books/Libros

A Fire Drill with Mr. Dill. Read-It! Readers (series). Susan Blackaby (Picture Window Books)

Learning How to Stay Safe at School. The Violence Prevention Library (series). Susan Kent (PowerKids Press)

Playing at School/Juego en la escuela. My Day at School/Mi día en la escuela (series). Joanne Mattern (Gareth Stevens Publishing)

School Safety. Living Well, Safety (series). Lucia Raatma (Child's World)

Seguridad cuando hay fuego. Kyle Carter (Rourke Publishers)

Who's Who in a School Community. Communities at Work (series). Jake Miller (PowerKids Press)

Index

Índice

About the Author

Joanne Mattern has written more than 150 books for children. She has written about weird animals, sports, world cities, dinosaurs, and many other subjects. Joanne also works in her local library. She lives in New York State with her husband, three daughters, and assorted pets. She enjoys animals, music, going to baseball games, reading, and visiting schools to talk about her books.

Información sobre la autora

Joanne Mattern ha escrito más de ciento cincuenta libros para niños. Ha escrito textos sobre animales extraños, deportes, ciudades del mundo, dinosaurios y muchos otros temas. Además, Joanne trabaja en la biblioteca de su comunidad. Vive en el estado de Nueva York con su esposo, sus tres hijas y varias mascotas. A Joanne le gustan los animales, la música, ir al béisbol, leer y hacer visitas a las escuelas para hablar de sus libros.